Featherstone

50

Series editor
ALISTAIR
BRYCE-CLEGG

fantastic things
to do with **mud and clay**

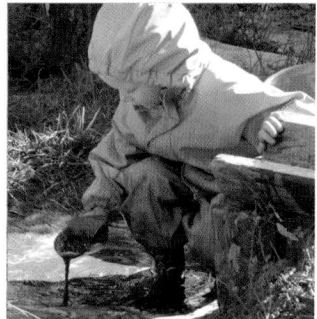

JUDIT HORVATH

Featherstone
An imprint of Bloomsbury Publishing Plc

50 Bedford Square
London
WC1B 3DP
UK

1385 Broadway
New York
NY 10018
USA

www.bloomsbury.com

Bloomsbury is a registered trademark of Bloomsbury Publishing Plc

First published 2017

British Library Cataloguing-in-Publication Data
A catalogue record for this book is available from the British Library.

ISBN:
PB 978-1-4729-4159-6
ePDF 978-1-4729-4158-9

Library of Congress Cataloging-in-Publication Data
A catalogue record for this book is available from the Library of Congress.

10 9 8 7 6 5 4 3 2 1

Printed and bound in India by Replika Press Pvt. Ltd.

This book is produced using paper that is made from wood grown in managed, sustainable
forests. It is natural, renewable and recyclable. The logging and manufacturing processes
conform to the environmental regulations of the country of origin.

To view more of our titles please visit www.bloomsbury.com

Contents

Introduction

The main aim of the book

When given a piece of ordinary soil, mud or clay most children are instinctively motivated to explore and experiment with it. The qualities of these materials make the handling experience magical for children; clay and soil respond and change in a unique way when touched, pressed, poked, squeezed or mixed with other materials. When playing with mud or clay children are naturally fascinated, motivated, and empowered to persevere, think creatively, use their imaginations and play autonomously. These materials are naturally open-ended, stimulating children to investigate possibilities, look for reasons and think of ideas. They are cheap and easy to source or access, simple to transform to suit any age group or activity, can be mixed with other materials, and give a rich sensory experience through visual texture, deep colour, rich smell and tactile feel.

The main aim of the book is to provide ideas on how this cheap and easily accessible material can be used effectively with early years children.

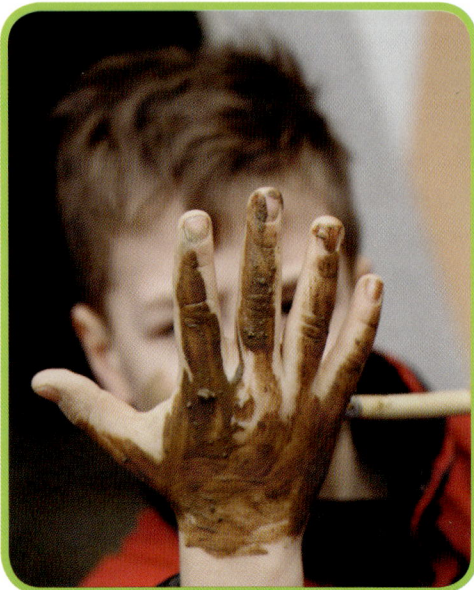

Learning through mud, clay and soil

Views and approaches about using mud with children have formed and transformed as centuries and circumstances change, but one thing has remained the same: children simply love mud! Mud is an underrated but creative and versatile material, perfect for complex learning. It can be used for a large variety of purposes, from building to beauty, as well as playing, healing and making art.

With our changing attitude towards nature and sustainability, mud certainly has value as an educational resource. Mud connects children with nature; there is a direct psychological effect and immediate environmental awareness. It really is true that mud can make people happier and healthier; research (lead by Chris Lowry at University of Bristol) has shown that natural dirt contains a harmless, microscopic soil bacterium that increases the levels of serotonin in the brain, helping soothe and calm, and improve cognitive functions.

With its direct effects on the brain, being a sensory activity, playing in mud does develop children intellectually. It can be an indoor or outdoor activity. It is a wonderful art medium because it responds in a variety of ways. It is mouldable, dries hard, can be used dry and wet and is perfect on its own but can also be mixed with other materials. Mud permits mistakes and still guarantees success, and it is inviting, challenging, and exciting. In some ways, mud also encourages children to gain a deeper understanding of what's around them as it develops their relationship with nature and the three-dimensional world. Children begin to understand shape, form, and perspective, learning to really look, see and discover their place in the world.

The structure of the book

The pages are all organised in the same way. Before you start any activity, read through everything on the page so you are familiar with the whole activity and what you might need to plan in advance.

What you need lists the resources required for the activity. These are likely to be readily available in most settings or can be bought/made easily.

What to do tells you step-by-step what you need to do to compete the activity.

Observation questions prompt the practitioner to evaluate how the children are engaging with one another and the activity itself, with links to the EYFS Statutory Framework.

The **Health & Safety** tips are often obvious, but safety can't be overstressed. In many cases there are no specific hazards involved in completing the activity, and your usual health and safety measures should be enough. In others there are particular issues to be noted and addressed.

Taking it forward gives ideas for additional activities on the same theme, or for developing the activity further. These will be particularly useful for things that have gone especially well or where children show a real interest. In many cases they use the same resources, and in every case they have been designed to extend learning and broaden the children's experiences.

Finally, **What's in it for the children?** tells you (and others) briefly how the suggested activities contribute to learning.

Mud puddle race

What you need:

- Adult- and child-sized spades
- Plain, soil covered area
- Welly boots
- Waterproof clothing
- Hose connected to a tap, or a bucket of water

What to do:

1. Dig a flat hole in the ground.

2. Use a hose, or pour a bucket of water on to the soil-covered area to soften.

3. Repeat the process until the soil is unable to absorb anymore water and a puddle forms.

4. For a jumping competition prepare at least two puddles.

5. Point out the hazards before starting the activity, especially when using natural puddles in common areas: road safety – when for example playing in a park; contaminated water – for example with engine oil floating on it; very deep puddles.

6. Divide the children into two teams and ask them to stand in two parallel lines.

7. Runners must run towards the puddle, jump over it and then return to tag the next person in their team to do the same. First team to finish wins!

What's in it for the children?

Children will enjoy each other's company whilst learning about taking turns, co-operation and working in a team.

Taking it forward

- Children can compete against each other based on who can jump higher.
- The relay race can involve jumping into the puddle rather than over it (check with parents first!).

Observation questions

- How does the child control his or her movements?
- Can the child concentrate and take turns?
- Is the child showing a developing stamina?

Health & Safety

Ask children to remove any jewellery and glasses before this activity. Put on boots and waterproof clothing as required.

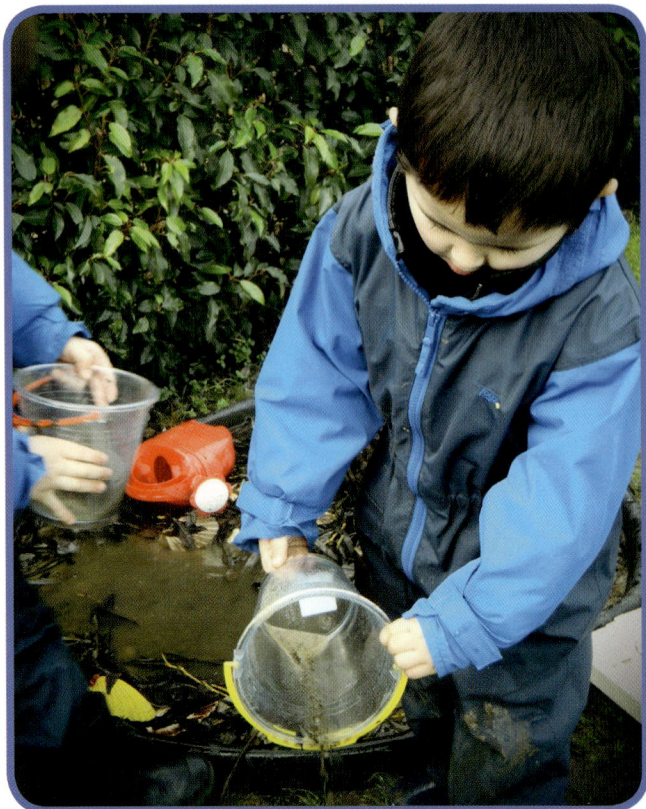

Find your own clay

Physical development

What you need:

- Adult- and child-sized spades
- Buckets
- Plain, soil covered area
- Welly boots
- Waterproof clothing
- Hose connected to a tap, or a bucket of water

What to do:

1. Find a spot outside, ideally in a park and create a large hole (if it is very near your setting, spray the area using a hose; if it is far away, try this activity after a rainy day).

2. Once the ground is wet, look around and see if you can find some orangey, yellow clumps. These will usually be covered with dirt but because the ground is now wet, they will be easier to find. Pick up one of these clumps: this is clay!

3. If the clay is covered with leaves, stones or other dirt, wash it with water and dry it slightly.

4. Let the children use it, moulding it as they would normal clay. Give them the opportunity to squeeze it and shape it exploring its properties fully.

What's in it for the children?

Children will begin to develop advanced muscle control and body strength.

Taking it forward

- Alternative modelling clay can be made from:
  - 720 g flour
  - 200 g salt
  - 450 ml water

Observation questions

- How does the child manipulate materials?
- How does the child control tools? One-handed or two-handed? Does the child use one hand mostly? If so, which one?

Health & Safety

If the clay contains debris which might be irritating to the children you will need to remove this in advance.

Spaghetti and clay buildings

Physical development

What you need:

- Slab of clay
- Piece of wire (optional)
- Dry spaghetti
- String, tape (optional)
- Scissors

What to do:

1. Cut the clay into assorted pieces (the easiest way to do this is with a piece of wire).

2. Knead the clay to make it soft and malleable.

3. Shape it into squares.

4. Make a sketch of a tower, based on the children's ideas.

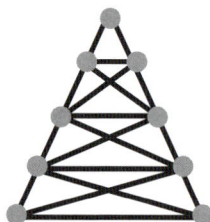

5. The dry spaghetti provides the framework and support for the tower, and the clay cubes can be used to make the connectors.

6. First prepare the basic shape and create as many sides as required. For example, when building a triangular tower create the three sides first, flat on a steady surface, then once each side is slightly set, link it together with additional clay cubes. Break the pieces of spaghetti to size if needed.

7. Once ready, leave the composition to dry.

What's in it for the children?

Children will use fine motor control and hand-eye co-ordination. They will also use their sense of balance whilst building.

Taking it forward

- Provide additional materials and set the challenge of building as high a tower as possible in a limited amount of time.

- Organise an exhibition of the completed structures.

Observation questions

- How does the child control their own body?

- Does the child show a preference for a dominant hand?

Mudhill climbing

Physical development

What you need:

- Tools to gather soil
- Large rocks
- Wooden logs
- Car tyres
- Soil
- Dry leaves
- Turf
- Gravel

What to do:

1. Collect together a variety of rocks, logs and car tyres to create a secure pile.

2. Cover it tightly with soil, then gravel, and finally turf.

3. Make sure it's safe and secure; try it before letting children climb onto it.

4. Alternatively, place long thick sticks into the pile to create support for the children to hold onto.

5. Place the tyres vertically and fill with soil on the bottom and sides to create a simple, low-cost, hill-like climbing structure.

6. Allow the children free play to explore the mud hill. Encourage them to reach and stretch across it.

What's in it for the children?

Children gain physical strength, balancing skills and stamina.

Taking it forward

- Log piles may be used for wildlife hibernation and nesting and will attract insects, snails and caterpillars, so they can be used for wildlife spotting.

Observation questions

- Can the child use his/her whole body and control his/her movements?

Health & Safety

Make sure the area is safe before allowing the children access to it.

Waterfalls and muddy channels

Physical development

What you need:

- Spades
- Multi-shaped, multi-coloured rocks
- Evenly shaped, smooth, shiny, large pebble type rocks
- Uniform large rocks
- Base and rubber liner in required size
- Gravel
- **Hose** (next to a water source)
- Sand/mud

What to do:

1. Choose a location. Install a waterfall on a natural slope or hill, or dig out the slope manually. If the soil or foundation is difficult to excavate, consider building the stream above ground using a combination of rocks and gravel as the base. The absolute minimum slope would need to be a 5 cm drop for every 3 metres of stream. The steeper the slope, the faster the water runs and the louder the sound of the waterfall.

2. Place the waterfall near a water source; if a natural source isn't available a hose can be hidden behind the pile of rocks. When putting the waterfall together, consider how to create a layering effect for the water to fall down, arranging the rocks around the sides and in the flow of the water.

3. Start excavating the foundation. Dig out any part of the stream that will be below ground. Dig out a large enough area for the lower sump basin, making sure to leave space for surrounding gravel and stone. Finally, place medium-sized rocks and larger boulders around the perimeter of the stream to hem it in.

4. Measure out and cut both underlay and rubber liner. Starting with underlay and then finishing with the liner, stretch them over the entire distance of the waterfall, into the lower basin, and across the base pond (if there is one). Place some of the rocks on the membrane plastic to hold it in place.

5. Layer gravel carefully across the bottom of any exposed surfaces of the liner.

6. Turn on the garden hose and spray down the entire area of the stream until the water level in the bottom basin is full.

7. For an ongoing feature use a pump to circulate the water (back up to the top) built inside the pile of rocks, or hide the hose ending at the top within the rocks.

8. If a pump is used, run the hose from the water pump, carefully hide the hose under the liner, and be sure to check for kinks. Check the flow of water before covering over the hose and liner.

9. Carefully check the water level and the water flow constantly.

10. On the bottom of the waterfall dig a small area next to the bottom basin and cover it with foil. Place some earth and sand in it to create a mud pit for the children. Encourage them to make drip sand castles. Provide spades, small guttering and/or other pipes and encourage the children to connect the bottom basin with the mud pit.

What's in it for the children?

The children will have opportunities to exercise and learn about their physical state whilst also gaining interesting, factual knowledge about waterfalls.

Taking it forward

- Visit real streams and waterfalls if there are any nearby.

Observation questions

- Does the child show signs of developing physical skills?

- Can the child manipulate tools skillfully?

Clay textures

Physical development

What you need:

- Slab of clay
- Piece of wire (optional)
- Rolling pin
- Different textures: pieces of fabric, sponge, dish scourer, textured rolling pins, leaves, texture mats, string, dowel rods

What to do:

1. Cut pieces of the clay (the easiest way to do this is with a piece of wire).

2. Knead the clay to make it soft and malleable.

3. Make small flat discs of clay by rolling a small ball between your palms and then flattening it with a rolling pin.

4. Whilst the clay is still soft, show the children how to carve or press patterns into it.

5. Alternatively, wrap string, twine or rope around a dowel in straight or criss-cross patterns. Roll over the clay.

6. Once ready, leave the compositions to dry.

What's in it for the children?

Clay stimulates the child's curiosity and many new neurons and brain synapses are generated when a child is engaged with the immediate tactile and visual feedback provided by clay. Manipulating a piece of clay develops the children's large and small muscles, whilst fostering eye-hand coordination.

Taking it forward

- Make small textured tiles and create a mosaic.
- Make and sell art pieces to support a charity.

Observation questions

- Can the child apply pressure?
- Can the child control their large muscles to manipulate objects?
- How are the children using their fingers? (This is good preparation for future writing and developing fine motor skills.)

Barefoot walk

Physical development

What you need:

- An outdoor area with a **variety of surfaces** (such as soil, grass, pebbles, bark etc.)
- **Markers such as rope, ribbon, scarves**
- **Wet wipes and towels**
- **Add a selection of natural extras: hay, gravel, leaves, sand**

What to do:

1. Create a walkway with a variety of safe surfaces and mark the area clearly for the children.
2. Discuss the walk and what they might experience (in terms of surprising surfaces and temperatures).
3. Remove shoes and socks.
4. Ask the children to walk slowly on the prepared surface.
5. Ask children (who are old enough to explain) to describe the feeling of the different textures. Which ones did they like?

What's in it for the children?

Apart from having fun when walking barefoot safely, it helps muscles develop, allows the skin to breathe, and feeling the ground beneath them will help the children learn to be confident on their feet.

Taking it forward

- Make textured walks indoors (ask the children to help you build them).

Observation questions

- Does the child show increasing strength?

✚ Health & Safety

Have a good supply of wet wipes and towels available to clean feet off afterwards!

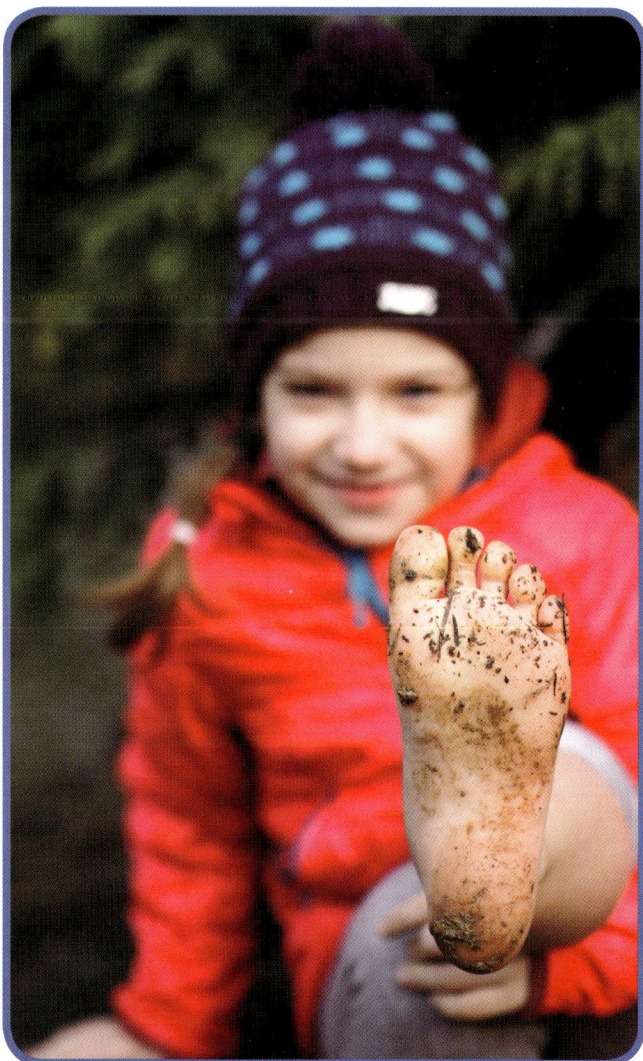

Soil skittles

Physical development

What you need:

- **Plastic drinks bottles**
- **Soil**
- **Kitchen funnel** (or make one with a cone of paper)
- **PVA** (white glue)
- **Acrylic paints and paintbrushes** (optional)
- **Ball to play**

What to do:

1. Collect together a number of plastic drinks bottles, preferably of the same size and shape.

2. Using a funnel, fill each bottle about one third full of earth (dirt) or any weighty soil. Paint around the top of the bottle with the glue and screw the lids on tightly.

3. Paint numbers on the bottles so they can be used for a scoring game.

4. Now line them up next to each other, grab a ball and roll it, trying to hit as many bottles as possible. Let the children take turns and see who gets the best score.

What's in it for the children?

The average skittle player uses over 100 muscles during the basic game by lifting, swinging, aiming, throwing. It is a weight-bearing activity which helps build strong healthy bones. The game requires mental focus and helps develop discipline. It also provides an exercise option for those with physical limitations.

Taking it forward

- Build side bars from simple large wooden blocks to enable younger children to enjoy the activity.

Observation questions

- Does the child show balancing skills?
- Is the child able to physically focus/concentrate to master aiming at the skittles?

Mud masks

Personal, social and emotional development

What you need:

- A teaspoon of bentonite clay or a small amount of any very clean, skin safe clay or soil
- Some honey
- Some warm water
- Dried, powdered flower such as chamomile, rose or lavender (best if collected with children)
- Dried, powdered herbs
- Two drops of olive oil
- Small mixing bowl
- Spoon
- Wash cloth and warm water

What to do:

1. Talk about how mud is used as a face mask because it has properties that can be good for the skin.
2. Mix the bentonite clay with the powdered herbs (if using) in a small bowl.
3. Add honey and mix to form a thick paste.
4. Add enough warm water to form a thin paste. Add the olive oil (if using).
5. Immediately apply to face and neck in a circular motion, avoiding the eyes.
6. Leave on for a couple of minutes or until it has hardened.
7. Wash off with a wash cloth soaked in warm water (really warm water helps to steam off the mask without having to rub the skin).
8. Pat skin dry and get the children to admire their smooth skin!
9. Talk about how the mask felt on their faces.

What's in it for the children?

Children gain an understanding about the importance of self-care.

Taking it forward

- Organise a spa day with a mud bath for their feet!
- Help the children set up an outdoor mud beauty salon.

Observation questions

- Does the child show an understanding of pretend play?
- Does the child make choices and express likes or dislikes?

Health & Safety

If used in an educational setting, always ask for specific permission from the parents to apply the mud mask on their children. Be aware of any skin allergies or conditions.

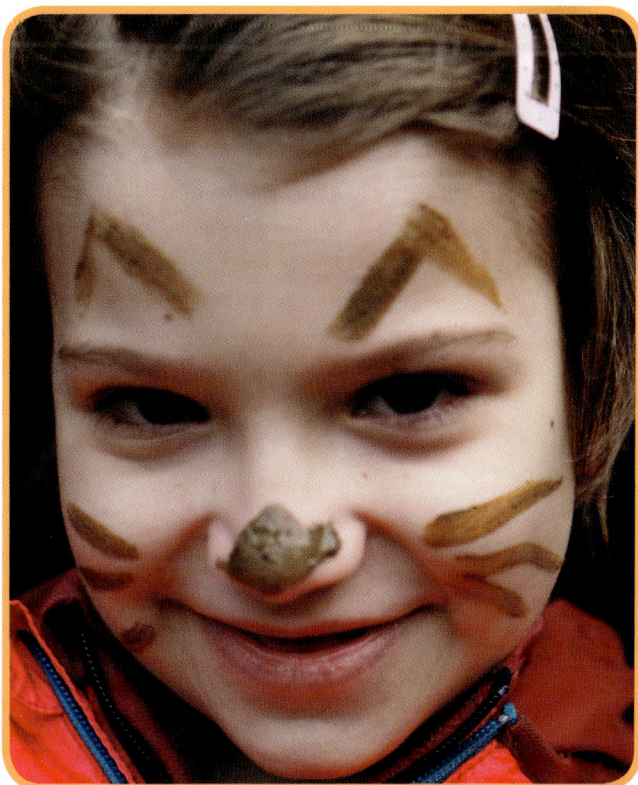

Body paint

Personal, social and emotional development

What you need:

- A piece of clay or some clean soil
- Water
- Buckets
- Large, soft brushes
- Soft sponges

What to do:

1. Place the soil or clay in the bottom of the buckets and start to add water.
2. Mix thoroughly, until a thick paste forms – this is the mud paint.
3. Encourage children to expose their legs and arms for painting.
4. Use the sponges and brushes to paint their arms and legs, they can paint themselves or work together to paint each other.
5. Take photos of the children when they are painted and make a display.
6. Alternatively, create an outline of the children on a large piece of paper and paint the silhouette with the mud paint.

What's in it for the children?

Children gain an understanding of their own physical being and their limitations. Through this sensory experience they will grow physical confidence and become comfortable with their own bodies. This will aid their social skills when they are in close proximity to others.

Taking it forward

- Throw a mud party.
- Create mud-painting portraits.

Observation questions

- Does the child show confidence in their own body?
- Does the child display an understanding of personal boundaries?

✚ Health & Safety

Always check with parents first before carrying out body painting activites, and be aware of any skin allergies or conditions.

My body prints

Personal, social and emotional development

What you need:

- A piece of clay
- Rolling pins
- Circle/square shaped cookie cutters
- Small plastic containers lined with foil

What to do:

1. Place a piece of clay in front of each child. Show them how to roll it flat and cut out a circular disc or square.

2. Place the discs into a plastic container lined with foil.

3. Press in the child's chosen body part: hand, foot, fingers, toes, tip of the nose, forehead, knees, elbows all make interesting imprints.

4. Hold it for a short while and then pull the body part straight up.

5. Let the print dry for about an hour if you have used the mould before popping out, then let it dry completely for several hours.

6. Compare the finished pieces and try to guess the body parts.

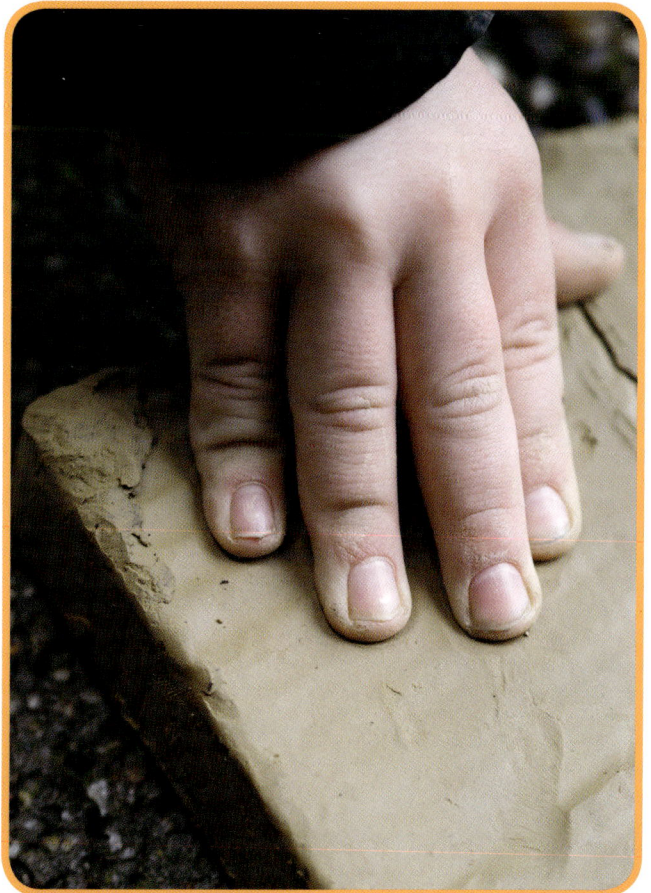

What's in it for the children?

Children gain an understanding of mark making and their own uniqueness.

Taking it forward

- Make imprints of household items and invite the children to guess what they are.

- Make a large mosaic 'person' on the wall out of the children's body part imprints.

Observation questions

- Does the child use different channels for self-expression?

- Does the child understand the similarities and differences between self and others?

My furry friend

Personal, social and emotional development

What you need:

- **A piece of clay** (preferably air drying)
- **Wire to cut**
- **Toothpick, small paintbrushes**
- **Water**
- **Clear reference pictures of birds** (showing the basic shape of the body and head)
- **Small feathers** (collect these with the children)

What to do:

1. Explain you are going to use clay to each make a bird. Have a look at the pictures together to get an idea of the basic shape.

2. Start with a lump of clay that fits in the hands. Show the children how to mould it until a ball is formed, then put it on the table. Carefully push down to flatten the bottom, without making holes on top of the ball.

3. Form a ball that is a bit smaller than a ping pong ball. Include a little extra (for the neck.) Put the head on top of the body at an angle, then smooth it in with some water. Use the extra to make a neck. To get this part right, keep a picture of a bird in view for the children to observe and copy.

4. Take a small rectangle of clay and put it opposite the head for the tail. Smooth it in.

5. Let the children add some detail. For the beak, locate the right place and put on a little bit of clay and smooth it in, then use a toothpick to shape the bird's mouth.

6. Make a clay oval and smooth it onto the side of the body. Use a toothpick to shape it. Do the same on the other side to make wings.

7. Show the children how to widen the tail at the end by lightly flattening and pushing into the clay. Make some ruffles by adding and smoothing in some clay strips the length of the tail.

8. Add eyes, using a toothpick.

9. Cover the whole model with a little bit of water and press on the feathers to cover the bird.

10. Leave to air dry. (Follow the instructions on the clay packaging to determine how best to dry the clay.)

➕ **Health & Safety**
Make sure any feathers the children handle are clean. Wash hands after modelling.

What's in it for the children?

Children gain an understanding of how to create for themselves and how to respect the belongings of others.

Taking it forward

- Name the clay creations and build a nest.
- Play vets using the children's clay pets.

Observation questions

- Can the child use his/her imagination to engage in pretend play?
- Does the child display a sense of pride?

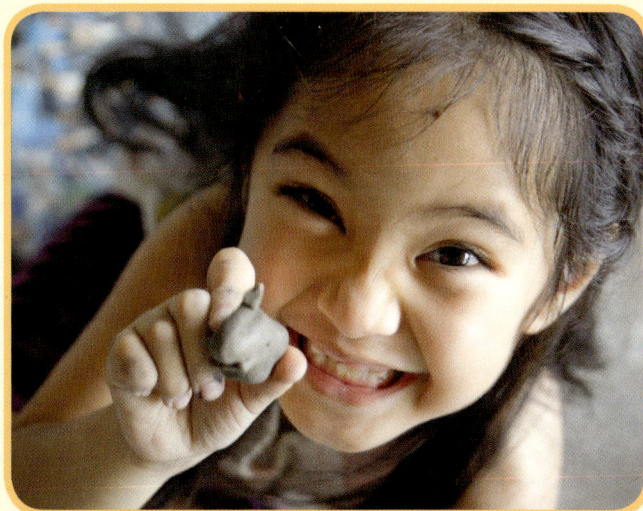

My number plate

Personal, social and emotional development

What you need:

- A piece of clay
- Wire to cut clay
- Small plastic containers lined with foil
- Plastic numbers and letters (cookie cutters)
- Photos of the children's home number plate /house name
- Embellishments (small pebbles, beads, shells etc.)

What's in it for the children?

Children gain an understanding of their own environment and that of others. They can discuss if they have visited each other's homes and their experiences there. They also learn about numerals and the importance of signs and symbols (such as street names, door numbers etc.).

Taking it forward

- Help the children to use plastic letters to make address plates as presents for their friends.

Observation questions

- Does the child know their own address?
- Does the child take part in the social interaction?

What to do:

1. During circle time, discuss where the children live and how houses and flat often have a number. Share the photos of different address plaques and try to compare them. Remain sensitive to individual children's situations and where they live.

2. Give a piece of clay to each child. Help them to roll it flat and cut a circular disc or square.

3. Place each disc into a plastic container lined with foil to use as a mould.

4. Use the plastic numbers to press in the child's house number, pressing slightly on all the details.

5. Hold it for a short while and then pull the number straight up to create a clear outline.

6. Add small embellishment such as clay coils, beads, small pebbles and shells.

7. Let it dry completely for several hours before popping it out.

8. Paint the finished pieces.

50 fantastic things to do with mud and clay

My Soil

Personal, social and emotional development

What you need:

- Samples of the soil from the environment in which the children live such as plant pots, garden, park, local forest etc.
- Small containers
- Tweezers, spoons
- Magnifiers
- Microscope
- Paper, colouring pencils (optional)

What to do:

1. Ask the children to bring soil samples from the immediate environment of their homes.

2. Place the children's samples into the small containers with their names on.

3. Compare the samples based on characteristics like thickness, colour, wetness, cleanliness etc, and discuss observations.

4. Continue exploring the samples with tools such as tweezers, magnifiers, microscopes and discuss with the children where the samples are from (in the case of smaller children encourage them to touch the soil).

5. Ask the children to draw pictures of the places where the soil is from.

What's in it for the children?

Children will be able to express their own views about their environment. They will gain additional information about where they live and the world around them.

Taking it forward

- Take similar samples of water or plants from the children's environments.
- Organise a soil discovery expedition around the setting.

Observation questions

- Is the child able to name places that are important to them?

Clay stick family

Personal, social and emotional development

What you need:

- A piece of clay
- Wire and wooden sticks
- Toothpicks, plastic knives
- Paint
- Thin paintbrushes
- Natural embellishments: pebbles, shells, leaves, grass, hay etc.
- Drawing or photograph of a doll

What's in it for the children?

Children can enjoy the sense of creation in their own way and at their own pace. They will be able to exercise fine muscle control, whilst also gaining a more developed ability to concentrate.

Taking it forward

- Organise a clay-stick people theatre performance.
- Make a clay-stick people picnic.

Observation questions

- Does the child understand that some things are theirs, some things are shared, and some things belong to other people?
- Can the child describe and give their own views using the creation?

✚ Health & Safety

Be vigilant with the children when using the wire and sculpting materials to avoid scratches or scrapes.

What to do:

1. Find a model such as a drawing or photo of a doll that the children can replicate. Clay dolls work best if kept small like dress-up dolls. Don't take on anything too complicated.

2. Make the frame: trim the sticks/wires until they are just about a centimetre longer than each section of the body. Wire or stick pieces will be needed for:
   - the upper and lower arms
   - the upper and lower legs
   - the feet, the hands
   - the head
   - the chest
   - the hips

3. Pad the frame with a cheap material such as aluminium foil and tape. Make the muscles by wrapping materials around the wire frame. Make sure to leave the extra wire uncovered, as this will be used to make the joints.

4. Roughly cover all of the padded areas with clay. If using an air-dry clay, work on only one body part at a time to preserve the softness of the clay.

5. Sculpt the details. Start adding more clay and carving other parts away to create details like eyes, nose, mouth, fingers, etc. Carve the clay with toothpicks, utility knives, empty pens etc.

6. Dry the clay then paint the detail: add eyes, stick on embellishments etc.

7. For young children make a simpler version: give them a piece of thicker stick and work a small ball of clay on as the head, finally ask them to decorate as they chose.

Mud café
Communication and language

What you need:

- A piece of clay
- Water
- Old cutlery and dishes
- Old mugs, teacups
- Old tablecloth
- Smaller, cut pieces of tree trunks or large logs
- A toy till
- Paper, pencil

What to do:

1. Choose an outdoor area (possibly with running water) and organise natural seating using logs and pieces of tree trunk. Create a seating circle and a separate kitchen/counter area for your café.

2. Mix the clay with water in small dishes.

3. Encourage the children to mould the clay on the dishes into the shape of cakes, sandwiches etc. as props for the café.

4. Set the remaining dishes, cups, plates, tablecloth in the fashion of a tea party and encourage the children to take their chosen role, such as waitress, guest, etc. to role play in their café.

What's in it for the children?

Children will be able to engage in the social situation and take on different roles. Their vocabulary will grow and their skills in self expression will develop.

Taking it forward

- Have a mud cake 'bake off'.

Observation questions

- Can the child initiate conversations?
- Can the child take part in pretend situations?

Make a small pond

Communication and language

What you need:

- A large container that will hold water
- Some gravel and rocks
- Soil
- Some small pond plants
- Pond liner or silicon (optional)

What to do:

1. Find or buy a large container such as a large washing-up bowl or a large pot. It needs to be strong enough to withstand the rigours of being outside, especially if it's frosty.

2. Put the container into the chosen place while it's empty (once it's full of water, it will be difficult to move). Ideally somewhere that gets a good amount of light, but isn't in full sunlight all day.

3. Sink it into the ground or leave it on the surface, but lower edges will help creatures to get in and out.

4. Seal any drainage holes (for example if using an old sink, silicon a plug into the plughole).

5. Put a layer of soil, then a layer of clean gravel in the bottom. Certain types of soil are full of nutrients and will prompt blooms of algae to form. Place logs around the edge to create stepping stones in and out of the pond.

6. Finally, fill the pond. Use rainwater from a water butt where possible. If not, use tapwater, although boil it first as the chlorine will need to evaporate.

7. Plant up the pond. Use a very low nutrient soil (special soil for ponds), mixed with grit. Submerged pondweed is vital to help the pond stay clear. Always use native plants. Pond creatures are great at finding ponds themselves.

8. Make sure the area is safe. Decide if it needs to be fenced off, otherwise clearly mark it.

9. Observe the pond at intervals and see which creatures have taken up residence there.

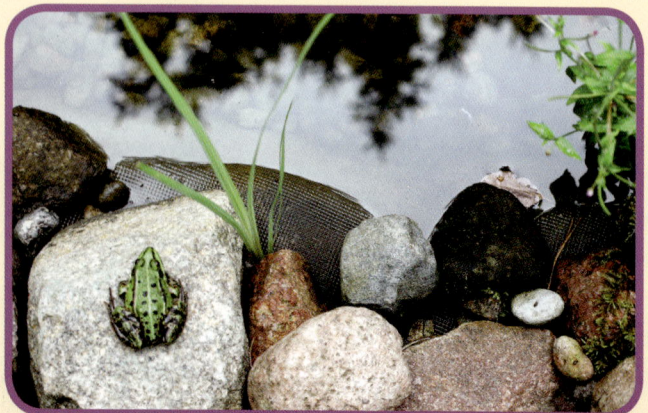

✚ Health & Safety

Warn children about the risks of playing around water and always supervise them.

50 fantastic things to do with mud and clay

What's in it for the children?

Children have the opportunity to discuss their experience when observing, comparing and spotting wildlife, using colourful descriptive language modelled by their leaders.

Taking it forward

- Visit a real pond, do pond dipping and examine the sludge.

- Create artificial sludge: 1 kg of cornflour, 2 ltrs water, 250 g rice (for bits and pieces that can be found in sludge) and brown food colouring.

Observation questions

- Does the child use a variety of words to describe their experiences?

Magical mud
Communication and language

What you need:

- A large bucket
- Dirt
- Water
- Baking soda
- Vinegar
- Powdered tempera paint, food colouring, or crushed chalk (optional – use if colour is desired)
- Spoons
- Old muffin trays
- Small dishes

What to do:

1. Mix all the ingredients (apart from the vinegar) in a large bucket.
2. Essentially all that is needed to transform plain mud into magical mud is the addition of vinegar.
3. Once the mud is all mixed up, it will look just like plain old mud.
4. Children can then have a bowl of the mud to play and make mud pies, cakes, muffins, and more!
5. Once the mud pies are ready, sprinkle with additional powder paint and baking soda, then pour vinegar onto it and wait for the magic to happen.

What's in it for the children?

Children are able to observe processes of basic chemistry (dilution, mixing), the connection between cause and effect and draw conclusions based on their own experiences.

Taking it forward

- Make a volcano by creating a deep hole in a mud pile and pouring the mixture of baking soda, red and yellow powder paint and vinegar into it.

Observation questions

- Do the children learn new words quickly when engaged in a new situation?
- Do the children ask questions when encountering unusual experiences?

Texture test
Communication and language

What you need:

- A long piece of fabric or a scarf
- Plastic containers
- Different types of dirt: soil, sand, gravel, sludge, clay, leaves, wood-pieces

What to do:

1. Show the children the different types of dirt and discuss their specific qualities such as texture, colour, smell etc.

2. Place them in small containers in a row, and use the scarf/fabric to blindfold the children, one at a time.

3. Hold the samples in front of them, asking them to smell and touch them, and to try to guess what they are.

4. Talk about the different textures and why they think which one is which. Encourage the use of descriptive words and expressions.

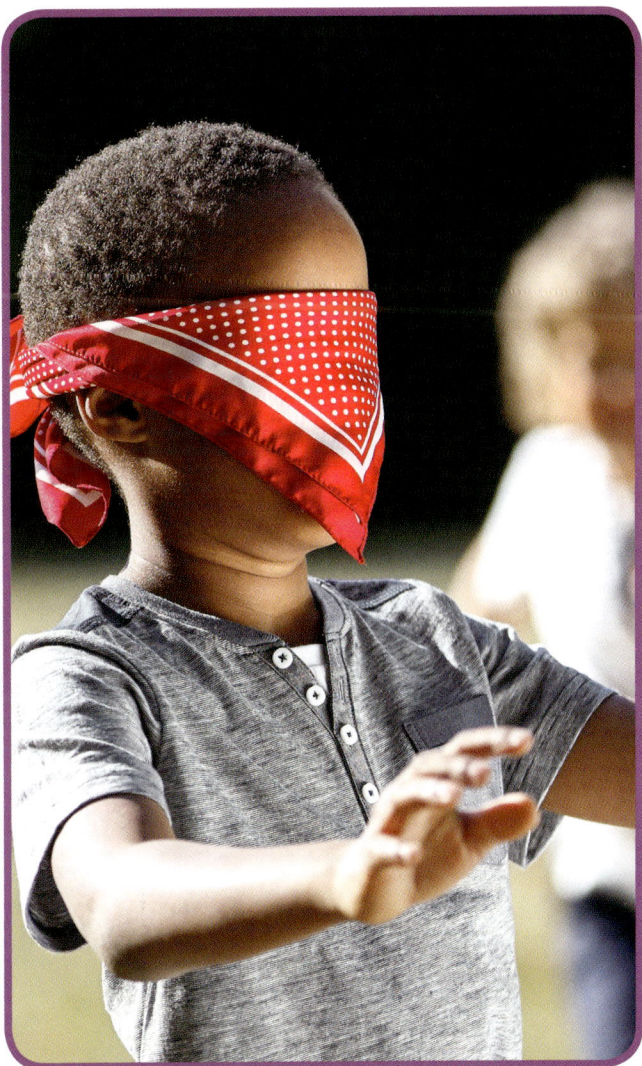

What's in it for the children?

Children will be able to use their senses to experience the world around them and gain information.

Taking it forward

- Go on a foraging trip to see what grows in the local soil, and organise a smell and taste test.

Observation questions

- Can the children communicate their thoughts?

- Can the children use their language skills to reason, organise and make decisions?

✚ Health & Safety

Always make sure children wash their hands thoroughly after handling the different materials.

Edible mud

Communication and language

What you need:

- Food processor
- Oatmeal
- Cocoa powder
- Cinnamon, cloves
- Oreos or other very dark sandwich biscuit
- Edible gummy worms
- Milk to mix
- Plastic cups
- Spoons

What to do:

1. Place all of the ingredients (except gummy worms) in a food processor or electric mixer and blitz until a breadcrumb-like texture is formed.

2. To make the perfect consistency, add some milk.

3. Share the mixture between the children using small transparent plastic cups and place gummy worms on the top of the 'mud'.

4. Discuss the similarities and difference between the characteristics of edible and real soil. Eat up the mud and worms!

What's in it for the children?

Children will be able to use their observation skills and descriptive language when comparing items that might look exactly the same.

Taking it forward

- Create sugar paste vegetables to add to the edible soil.
- Make a chocolate mud cake and cover it with edible soil.

Observation questions

- Can the children express their own observations?

Health & Safety

Be aware of any food allergies or intolerances before starting this activity.

Clay tiles
Mathematics

What you need:

- Piece of clay
- Wire to cut clay
- Pieces of recycled wooden planks/slats
- Handsaw
- Hammer and nails
- Strong plastic knives (or specialist potter's wooden knife)
- Varnish
- Sand, mud, tiny pebbles/ gravel

What's in it for the children?

Children can gain knowledge of sizes, differences and similarities. Understanding of size, shape and patterns is an early mathematical concept on which the mathematics curriculum is built.

Taking it forward

- Play guess the weight by preparing different sized clay balls, then use scales to check the accuracy of estimates.
- Make different sized wooden bird houses and decorate them with the clay tiles.

Observation questions

- Does the child show interest in numbers?
- Does the child use numbers in their communication?
- Does the child notice numerals in the environment?
- Does the child understand basic mathematical language such as bigger, smaller, more, less?

What to do:

1. Discuss sizes with the children during circle time using descriptive mathematical language such as small, tiny, large, huge, medium etc. and try to compare objects.

2. Make a variety of bottomless wooden frames: cut equal lengths of wooden slats and attach them to each other with nails.

3. Place a piece of clay in front of each child and press the clay into the frames, then cut away the excess clay.

4. Add small details and embellishment such as clay coils, beads, small pebbles, shells, then allow the clay to dry slightly.

5. Push the clay out of the frame using a strong material, a similar size to the tile.

6. Let the tiles dry completely for several hours.

7. Mix the varnish with sand, mud or small pebbles and paint the finished pieces.

8. Ask the children to line up the tiles by size. They can place numbers on them if they wish to.

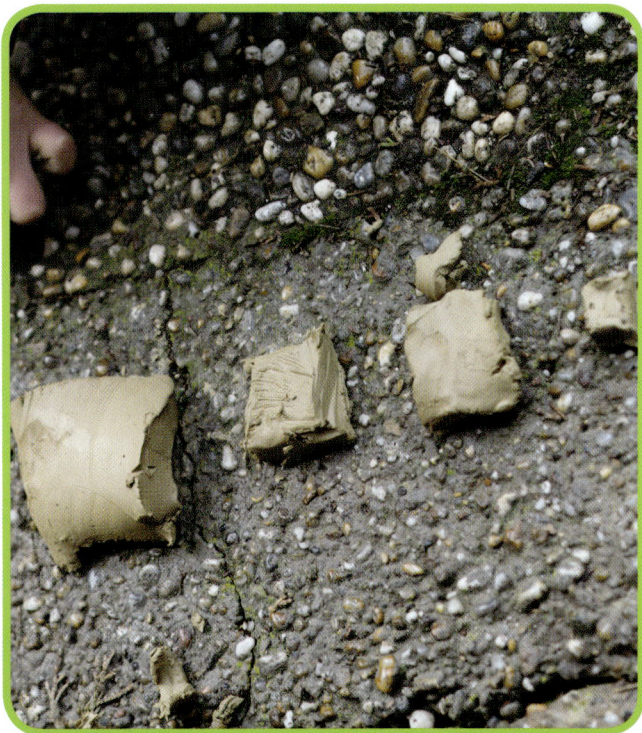

Small world soil maze
Mathematics

What you need:

- Builder's tray or a very large shallow container
- Play figures
- Soil
- Sand
- Moss, leaves, sticks, fern and other small plants
- Corks
- Natural additions such as pine cones, conkers

What to do:

1. Discuss the scene that you will create together (either a forest, park, woodland or neighbourhood) and ask the children to draw sketches to plan their ideas.

2. Place the builder's tray/container safely on a table or on the ground.

3. Scatter soil in the bottom of the tray, then create a maze by carving out different routes with your finger.

4. Work alongside the children as they play and encourage them to create their environment, planting small plants and using the natural materials. Add play characters.

5. Allow plenty of space for the children to develop their ideas.

6. Encourage children to think imaginatively and to find items to represent other objects, for example, a twig from the outdoor area to use as a tree.

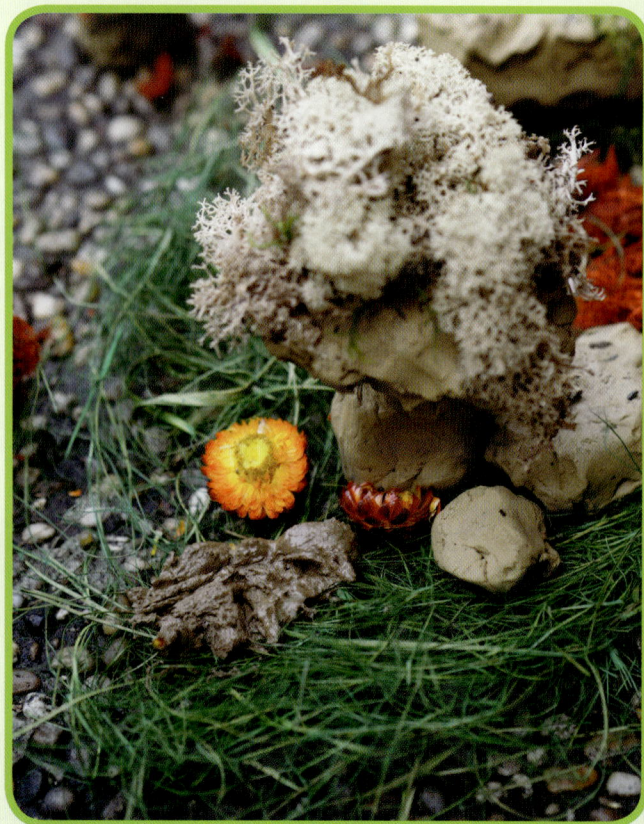

50 fantastic things to do with mud and clay

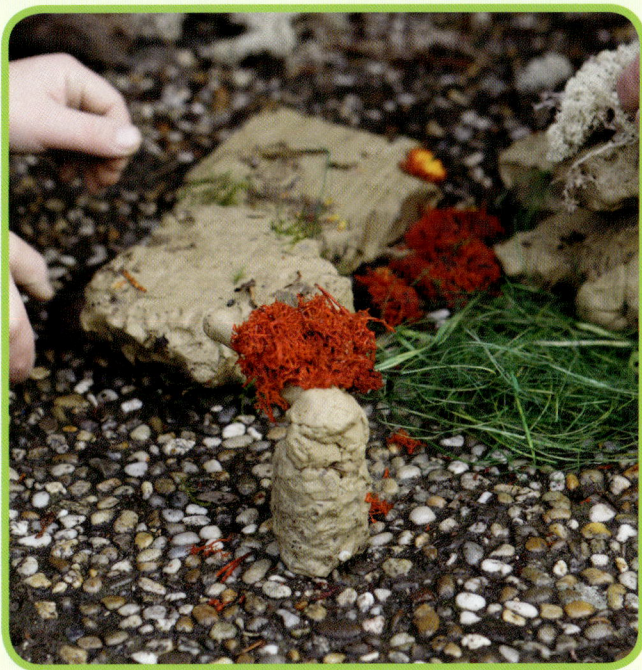

What's in it for the children?

Children will be able to select equipment to build and develop their environments, work alone or co-operatively, talk about their ideas and negotiate roles with others. They will use language to link ideas and recreate experiences, explore concepts of space and size, make maps and plans, become deeply involved in play, and develop ideas and understanding over a period of time.

Taking it forward

- Make a life-sized maze outdoors from large cardboard boxes.

- Make maze maps.

Observation questions

- Can the children work as a part of a group?

- Do the children know any shapes?

- Do the children show an understanding of basic concepts?

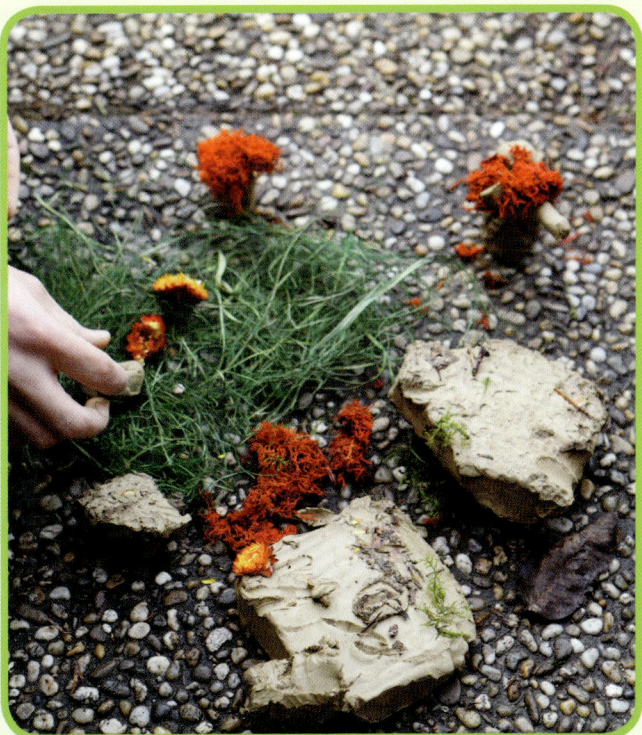

50 fantastic things to do with mud and clay

Underground plumbing

Mathematics

What you need:

- Newspaper
- Spades
- Mud
- Buckets
- Small plastic plumbing tubes, guttering, pipes
- Images of old and new plumbing systems, sewers

What's in it for the children?

Children will solve problems and understand the connection between space, forms and volumetric capacity.

Taking it forward

- Visit or look at images of a real old (e.g. Roman) water-system.

Observation questions

- Can the children prepare simple geometric drawings?
- Do the children show interest in listening to or expressing new knowledge?

What to do:

1. Discuss with the children what they know about plumbing and show them some informative pictures. Look at images of buildings and guess what is underneath them.

2. Make a plumbing plan: first designate and measure the area where the pipes will be placed, and create a sketch-base from newspaper (to mark out the size of the plumbing area). Gather the guttering, plumbing tubes etc. and lay these out on the floor (placing them on the newspaper sketch-base) and when the children are happy with the layout, ask them to roughly draw around everything.

3. Dig a shallow hole in the designated area.

4. Let the children build the plumbing system according to their original sketch using the guttering pieces.

5. Alternatively, lay some ends of the guttering at such an angle that children can pour water into their system. For extra excitement, cover the plumbing system with mud and let the children pretend to be plumbers.

Making mini bricks
Mathematics

What you need:

- Pictures of buildings
- Selection of shape building blocks
- A piece of clay
- Wire to cut clay
- Embellishments (small pebbles, beads, shells etc.)

What to do:

1. Discuss what shapes the children know, looking at examples in your room. Look at images of buildings and the materials they are made from.

2. Place a piece of clay in front of each child and ask them to divide it up into hazelnut-sized pieces.

3. Roll/form the pieces together gently to create shapes (cube, cuboid, cylinder, sphere) – the children can use the building blocks as examples.

4. Add small embellishments such as clay coils, beads, small pebbles, shells.

5. Let the bricks dry completely for several hours.

6. Paint or varnish the finished pieces.

7. Ask the children to build with the clay bricks.

What's in it for the children?

Children gain an understanding of geometric shapes, the notion of 3D, and by comparing objects within their environment, they can develop their observational skills.

Taking it forward

- Create other types of bricks and organise a *Three Little Pigs* play.

Observation questions

- Does the child pick up new mathematical language?
- Does the child express basic mathematical knowledge?

Make a soil castle
Mathematics

What you need:

- Soil
- Sand
- Buckets of water
- Mixing bowls and spoons

What to do:

1. Ask the children to draw plans for their castles.
2. Prepare a clear, flat surface outside.
3. Mix soil or sand and water to create a very thick paste.
4. Create the base of the castle with a mound of sand.
5. Start building the castle. Demonstrate how to grab a fistful of wet, 'slurry mud' and add it to the pile.
6. Drip the slurry over the creation by pointing the hand over it thumb down. Then let some of the mixture in the hand drip down through the other fingers.
7. Let the children use their plans to produce a castle.

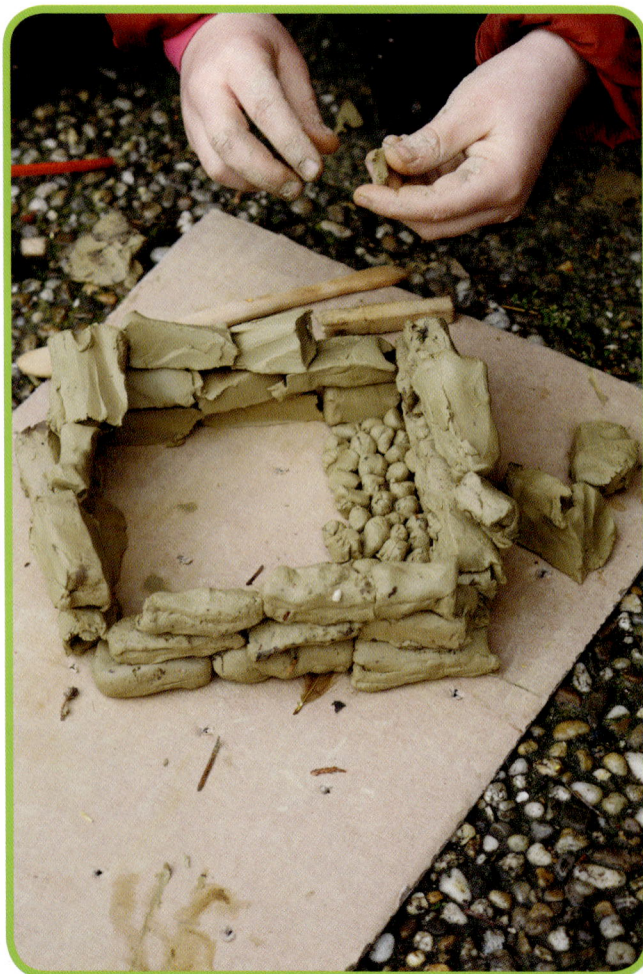

What's in it for the children?

Children develop spatial understanding and applied mathematical knowledge in a fun way.

Taking it forward

- Make drip castles from different basic ingredients: sand, plaster of Paris, etc.

Observation questions

- Does the child show enthusiasm for solving the problem?
- Does the child initiate/take part in discussions about mathematical problems?
- Does the child show awareness of similarities of shapes in the environment?
- Does the child talk about the qualities of the objects?

Pattern hunt
Mathematics

What you need:

- Clipboard
- Paper
- Pencil
- Camera

What to do:

1. Give the children a clipboard, pencil and piece of paper each and go for a walk in your environment. They will encounter a wide range of patterns on the soil/ in the mud.

2. Ask the children to draw the patterns they see, describe what sort of pattern it is and try to explain why the object has this pattern. Let them use a digital camera to record the patterns they find.

3. When gathered together back in the classroom, ask the children to: share their patterns and compare them with each other, classify them (e.g. various types of repeating or symmetrical patterns, natural or manufactured, precise or approximate etc.) and represent each different type of pattern using symbols, models or digital images.

4. Provide modelling materials for the children to recreate the patterns they have seen.

What's in it for the children?

Children can develop an understanding of patterns, repetition and how these occur in nature.

Taking it forward

- Make a pattern hunt of other natural things, such as plants, animals etc.
- Organise an indoor pattern hunt and compare indoor and outdoor patterns.

Observation questions

- Does the child pay attention to details?
- Can the child recognise similarities and differences?
- Does the child notice irregular arrangements?
- Does the child compare groups, characteristics?

Soil weighing
Mathematics

What you need:

- **Different types of soil, sand, clay**
- **Measuring jugs**
- **Scales** (provide both digital and analogue)

What to do:

1. Show the children the different types of soil. Encourage them to examine each type through touch, smell, observation (make sure no one tries to eat it!)

2. Fill the measuring jugs with the different types of soil to the same capacity, such as 100 ml.

3. Weigh the samples and discuss why the different types of soil might differ in weight.

What's in it for the children?

Children can gain an understanding of size, weight, capacity. They will learn about the similarities and differences in the characteristics of objects.

Taking it forward

- Weigh natural objects found in the mud or on the soil in a similar way. Measure things like shells, pebbles, sticks, leaves and feathers.

Observation questions

- Does the child show an interest in solving simple problems?

- Can the child understand that things can be counted, weighed or measured?

- Does the child estimate and then check by counting, measuring, weighing?

Clay numbers
Mathematics

What you need:

- A piece of clay
- Wire to cut clay
- Small number cookie cutters
- **Embellishments** (small pebbles, beads, shells etc.)

What to do:

1. During circle time discuss what numbers the children know, including their house number, the number of children in their group, the number of members in their families, how old they are, how many months are there, when they were born and so on.

2. Place a piece of clay in front of each child. Show them how to roll it flat and cut numerals from the clay.

3. Roll the leftover pieces together, and repeat the process.

4. Add small embellishment such as clay coils, beads, small pebbles, shells.

5. Let the numbers dry completely for several hours.

6. Paint or varnish the finished pieces.

7. Repeat the circle time discussion, using the clay numerals.

What's in it for the children?

Children develop an understanding of numerals. During the discussion they can learn new vocabulary, using their knowledge in a new context. Their visual understanding and simple expression of basic maths will grow.

Taking it forward

- Make clay dominoes.

Observation questions

- Can the child follow simple instructions?
- Does the child show interest in listening to or expressing new knowledge?

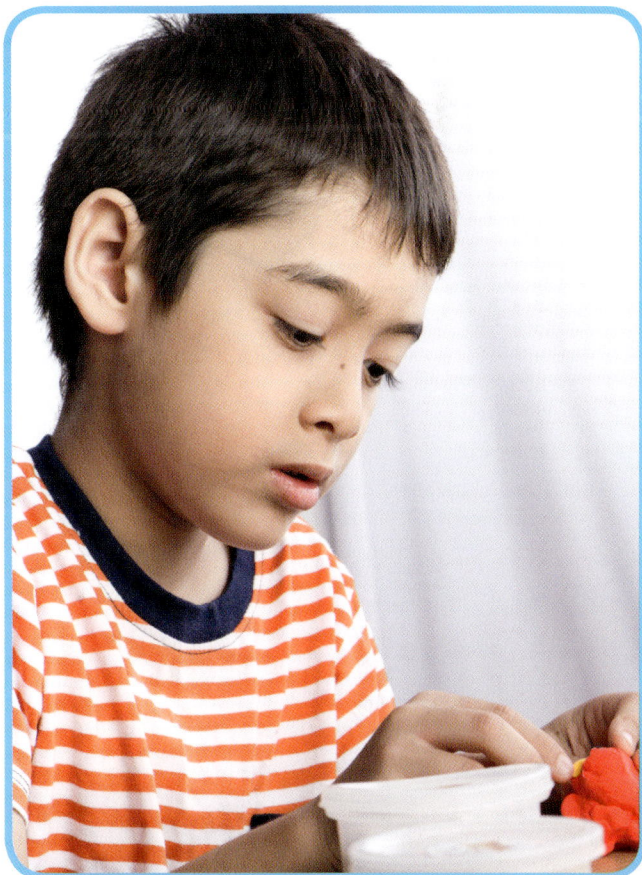

Garden signs

Literacy

What you need:

- Paper, pencil
- Wooden discs
- Leaves
- Wooden skewers, sticks
- String
- Paint made from crushed chalk, mud and water

What to do:

1. Walk around the garden/outdoor play area with the children and discuss the different characteristics of the area (sandy area, digging area, grassy area etc.)

2. Try to sketch a map that will help the children in preparing the signs.

3. To make the paint: mix four thumb-sized lumps of crushed chalk with 50g clay and add water gradually until you are happy with the consistency.

4. Paint onto the wooden discs or leaves to indicate areas.

5. Secure the discs or leaves onto the wooden sticks with string and hang in the relevant areas.

What's in it for the children?

Children can develop an understanding of the connection between print, words and meaning. They will be able to practise making marks.

Taking it forward

- Paint the children's names with chalk-mud paint.
- Make signs for the plants.
- Make signs with different symbols.

Observation questions

- Is the child interested in mark making?
- What is the child's preferred way to make marks?
- Is the child able to negotiate and listen to others?

Follow the trail

What you need:

- Paper
- Pencil
- Animal print tracking guide

What's in it for the children?

Children can use their observation and investigation skills, and learn about the importance of attention to detail. They will understand that marks/prints carry meaningful information.

Taking it forward

- Let the children make sets of prints for different creatures and lay trails for their friends to follow.

Observation questions

- Is the child interested in marks?
- What symbols does the child show interest in?

What to do:

1. Walk around in the chosen outdoor area and try to find animal prints in the muddy areas.
2. Find the clearest print and try to follow the trail.
3. Make a story about a day in the life of which animal the print belongs to.
4. Alternatively, make a set of prints in advance, place them in a trail and let the children follow the artificial trail.

Animal mark making

Literacy

What you need:

- Paper
- Pencil
- Camera
- Tape measure
- Animal print tracking guide

What's in it for the children?

Children can develop an understanding of connection between print, words and meaning. They will be able to practise making drawings to represent what they have seen.

Taking it forward

- Make a map of the area showing which animals live where, based on the animal marks the children found.
- Make an animal print guide.

Observation questions

- Is the child interested in marks?
- What symbols does the child show interest in?

What to do:

1. Walk around in the chosen outdoor area and try to find animal prints in the muddy areas.

   - Mammals will often leave more topographical prints, meaning that the prints sink to various depths in the surface of the earth. You may notice claws, individual toes, and foot pads in the prints of mammals.

   - Reptile tracks will generally be found around water, meaning they are usually quite smudged and obscured. Most reptiles leave five-toed prints and these are usually evenly pressed into the earth.

   - Birds generally leave three-toed prints, which are usually quite straight and bony.

2. Find the cleanest print. Identify the front and the back of the print.

3. Count the number of toes if any.

4. Estimate the length and width of the print. Use a tape measure for precise measurements.

5. Examine the shape of the print (hooved, four-toes, five-toed, variable).

6. Look for the presence of claws.

7. Take a picture of the print with a camera or make simple drawings and look for information about the print.

Mud notes

Literacy

What you need:

- Sticks
- Pebbles
- Water
- Objects found outdoors
- Dictaphone

What to do:

1. Walk around the chosen outdoor area and find different muddy areas.

2. Collect objects to create different noises by applying different forces on the surface (stepping, jumping, sliding, stomping, banging, tapping etc.).

3. Create and observe the different noises using imitative words such as dripping, squelching, oozing, clicking, buzzing, crackling, splashing etc.

4. Record the noises and play them back in circle time, trying to guess how the sound was created.

What's in it for the children?

Children can observe sounds and develop greater skills in understanding through listening.

Taking it forward

- Play sound bingo.
- Ask the children to record similar sounds in their own home environment and compare them in circle time.

Observation questions

- Do the children show attention to detail?
- Are the children talking about their experiences?

Secret messages from fairies
Literacy

What you need:

- Small paper box
- Potion ingredients (cookie crumbs, glitter, a small flower etc.)
- Glitter, toy jewellery
- Small ribbons
- Small make-up mirror
- Leaves
- Very thin brushes
- Mud, small plastic cups

What to do:

1. Put some toy jewellery, glitter and 'magic potions' etc. in a little fairy box as a hidden treasure.

2. Chose a muddy area to place it in and make the area pretty with glitter.

3. Invite the fairy to come in. Sprinkle a trail of crushed flower petals/leaves, small pieces of ribbons, leaves leading to the area so the fairy can get in and out easily.

4. Make loose mud in a plastic cup by diluting mud with water and write/paint a pictorial letter on a leaf.

5. Prepare a response letter to the children from the fairies.

6. Discuss the experience and encourage the children to tell a fairy story they know.

What's in it for the children?

Children can understand the connection between the printed storyline and actual events. They can practise mark-making.

Taking it forward

- Make a book based on the children's experiences.
- Use known stories such as Peter Pan.

Observation questions

- Does the child show understanding of prepositions such as 'under', 'on top', 'behind' when carrying out an action?
- Does the child engage in role play? What role does the child play?
- Does the child have book related memories/experiences?
- Does the child show interest/ask questions?

50 fantastic things to do with mud and clay

Soil stamping

What you need:

- Soil
- Sand
- Flour
- Water
- Clay
- Biscuit cutters
- An empty book or sugar paper sheets

What to do:

1. Mix the flour with the same quantity of soil or sand and add water to make a malleable dough. Alternatively, use clay.

2. Give each child a piece of dough or clay, ask them to roll or flatten it (if they want to) and place cookie cutters in front of them.

3. Ask the children to make marks by pressing the cutters into the dough, and discuss the end results.

What's in it for the children?

Children can observe the connection between print and meaning, they can make universal but personal marks.

Taking it forward

- Carve the children's names onto the soil-clay and create little name/initial pendants.

Observation questions

- Does the child respond to simple instructions about letters, for example to get or put away an object?

- Is the child able to follow, imagine print by description without pictures?

- Does the child use different ways to express opinion about their experiences such as body language, mimicking, sounds etc.?

D is for dirt

What you need:

- Garden tools, child-sized
- Paper
- Pencil
- An empty book or sugar paper sheets
- Camera

What to do:

1. Select an outdoor area that is suitable for gardening and prepare the area.

2. Sew some seeds at the appropriate time of the year – choose simple plants such as herbs, pre-grown strawberry, lettuce.

3. Whilst preparing for and actively engaging in gardening, find words related to the activity, starting with each letter of the alphabet. Make a list with the children for each letter and see which words they suggest.

4. Make notes of the objects, events and activities related to the letters that the children come up with and prepare an alphabet book together.

What's in it for the children?

Children can observe the connection between print and meaning. Through learning information by engaging in activities, they have the opportunity to develop life-long personal knowledge.

Taking it forward

- Make an indoor letter book or home letter book using the same principles.

Observation questions

- Do the children show interest in letters?

- Can the child link sound to letter or image?

- Is the child interested signs/ symbols? Does the child ask questions?

Soil colour mixing

Expressive arts and design

What you need:

- **Different types of soil** (from different places in the children's environment)
- **Small containers**
- **White and black card**
- **Paintbrushes**

What to do:

1. Show the different types of soil to the children.
2. Discuss how one colour can have many shades.
3. Set up the soil in small containers, mix water to create muddy paint.
4. Ask the children to create pictures on black paper that show the different shades of the soil colours.
5. Ask the children to mix the different coloured mud paints and create pictures on the white card that shows their freshly mixed colours.
6. Compare the pictures.

What's in it for the children?

Children can gain an understanding of connections, cause and effect, transformation.

Taking it forward

- Mix the mud paint with natural objects (such as grass, plants and leaves, pebbles, flower petals) and crushed chalk paint.

Observation questions

- Does the child select appropriate resources and adapt work where necessary?
- Does the child present original ideas?

Clay beads necklace

Expressive arts and design

What you need:

- Clay
- Plastic straws
- Plastic knife
- Paper towel
- Paint
- Wire, very thin
- Ribbon

What to do:

1. Give each of the children a piece of clay (rectangular if possible) and a plastic knife.

2. Use the knife to cut the clay into cubes.

3. Roll the cubes into small balls one by one. Encourage the children to make them as round as possible and different in lengths.

4. Pick them up carefully and poke a hole through the middle with a straw. If the straw gets full of clay, get another one.

5. Leave the balls out on a paper towel until they dry. It may need to be a few days, or it could even be a few weeks.

6. Paint them and let them dry again completely.

7. String the beads on a piece of thin wire. Make sure that about an inch on either end of the wire is left to close it off. Yarn can also be used, but wire is best to support the heavy beads.

8. Close off the wire: tie a loop on a piece of ribbon, drive the ribbon through the loop and, twisting the loose ends, fold them down flat. When using yarn, just tie a knot.

What's in it for the children?

Children can experience the joy of personal creation and making handmade gifts.

Taking it forward

- Make clay bracelets and pendants as gifts for families.

- Encourage the children to make repeating patterns by joining beads in different colour sequences.

Observation questions

- What materials does the child use?

- Does the child show preference when using different types of media?

Mud bakery

Expressive arts and design

What you need:

- **Play mud** (made from cornstarch, water, brown food colouring or cocoa powder)
- **Materials to add texture** (such as rice flour and baking soda)
- **Clay**
- **Crates, plastic tubs and boxes.**
- **Wooden spoons**
- **Whisks**
- **Muffin tray**
- **Bundt pan** (ring shaped mould)
- **Cookie sheets**
- **Measuring spoons and cups**
- **Buckets**
- **Large tub** (to act as a sink)
- **Nearby hose**

What to do:

1. Prepare the mud for the children's bakery:
   - Add the brown food dye to the water
   - Mix the cornstarch (approx 200g) with the water
   - Add 150g cocoa powder
   - One mixed, gradually add in water until the 'mud' is a consistency you're happy with.
   - For grittier/more realistic dirt, add in textured ingredients such as rice flour.

2. Set up the bakery: have a dough preparation/mixing station, a large plastic box for an oven, a large tub for a sink and a decoration table.

3. Place the suitable tools onto each station such as bowls and whisks on the dough preparation table, small tools on the decoration table etc.

4. Encourage the children to make leaf decorated pies, sand dusted mud cookies, a gravel sprinkled Bundt (ring cake) and ask them to create their own cake designs.

What's in it for the children?

Make believe play involves children recalling pictures they have built up in their mind from past experiences and using them in new, creative ways. In imaginary play children recreate scenes and practise solving problems creatively. In observing, discovering and carrying out deductive reasoning, pretend play is critical for creative thinking skills and helping children develop the ability to draw their own conclusions.

Taking it forward

■ Make a clay gingerbread house and sell it for charity.

Observation questions

■ Does the child make up stories?

■ Does child try different roles when engaging in pretend play?

Mosaic art with clay

Expressive arts and design

What you need:

- Piece of clay
- Wire to cut clay
- Small plastic containers lined with foil
- Paint/varnish
- Cement, water
- Tile adhesive
- Soft cloth
- Safety glasses
- Protective gloves
- Thin blanket or cover

What to do:

1. Introduce the idea of a mosaic with the children during circle time.

2. Place a piece of clay in front of each child. Roll it flat and cut a square disc or tile. Use paper/cardboard cut-outs as guides.

3. Let the tiles dry completely for several hours.

4. Paint the tiles and let them dry again.

5. Get an idea of what kind of mosaic the children would like to make. Encourage them to sketch a basic drawing of what they want it to look like when it is finished.

6. With safety glasses and protective gloves on, throw the tiles at any hard object, or simply drop them. In order to avoid scratches, lay a thin blanket on the ground.

7. Gather the broken tiles into colour and size categories. This will help when the time comes to actually put them into place.

8. Lay them onto the surface that will be decorated.

9. Individually glue each piece into place with the tile adhesive.

10. Once the tiles have set, mix up the cement with water until it is of the consistency described on the cement bag (liquid but not runny). Put the cement/water mix over all the tiles.

11. Using a soft cloth, rub off the excess cement that covers the tile pieces.

What's in it for the children?

Children can gain an understanding of different forms of expression. They can use their cognitive skills by thinking about alternative ways to communicate their thoughts through artistic media.

Taking it forward

- Visit a museum to get inspiration.
- Make a natural pebble mosaic.

Observation questions

- Does the child use a variety of media to express their thoughts?
- Does the child show pride in their work?

Dinosaur mini world

Expressive arts and design

What you need:

- Builder's tray or very large shallow container
- Soil, sand, pebbles
- Moss, leaves, sticks
- Rocks
- Fern and other small plants
- Corks
- Wooden discs (tree cookies)
- Natural additions such as pine cones, conkers
- Dinosaurs
- Small world characters

What to do:

1. Discuss a dinosaur mini world theme and ask the children to draw sketches.

2. Place the builder's tray/container safely on a table or on the ground.

3. Scatter soil around in the bottom of the tray, then organise the plantation.

4. Add play characters.

5. Allow plenty of space for the children.

6. Encourage children to think imaginatively and to find items to represent other objects, for example, a twig from the outdoor area to use as a tree.

What's in it for the children?

Children will be able to tell their own stories, talking about key characters and sequencing events. They can work alone or co-operatively, talk about their ideas and negotiate roles with others, whilst engaging in imaginative play.

Taking it forward

- Make clay dinosaurs to use in the play scene.
- Make clay trees.

Observation questions

- Does the child happily manipulate the materials?
- Does the child lead, listen or follow in the activity?

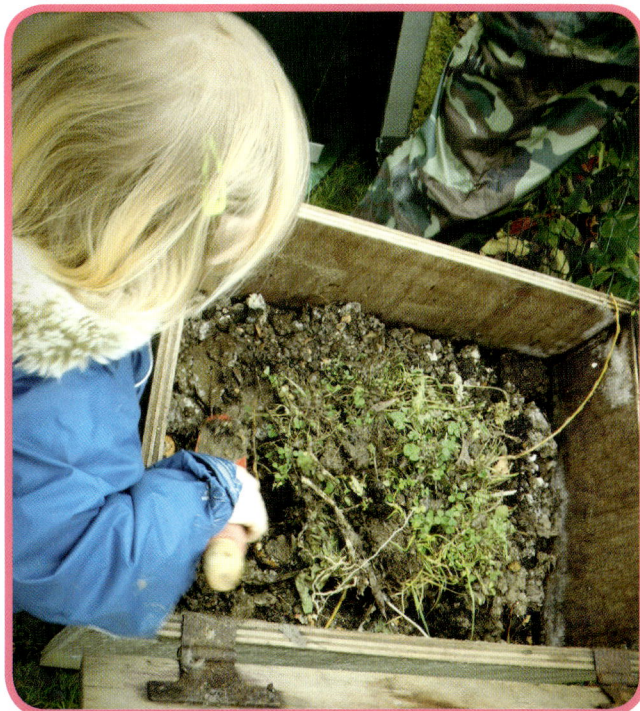

Clay windchimes

Expressive arts and design

What you need:

- Clay
- Plastic knife
- Paper towel
- Plastic straws
- Varnish, glitter
- Piece of wood, cardboard or plastic
- String
- Examples of windchimes

What to do:

1. Show the children a windchime as an example and talk about how it is used.

2. Explain that they are going to make their own windchime.

3. Give each of the children a piece of clay (rectangular if possible) and a plastic knife.

4. Let them use the knife to cut the clay into cubes.

5. Roll the cubes into long strips one by one. Encourage the children to make them as round as possible and different in lengths.

6. Pick them up carefully and poke a hole through one end with a straw. If the straw gets full of clay, use another one.

7. Leave the long strips out on a paper towel until they dry. It may need to be a few days, or it could be a few weeks.

8. Varnish them, dip them in glitter and let them dry again completely.

9. Make the wind chime base. This can be made from wood, metal or plastic and is usually circular. Add holes to allow for tying the chimes on.

10. Decide the required length of the chimes.

11. Knot the string at the top of the base hole. Tie the other end of the string through the hole of a chime.

12. Insert three hooks at even intervals across the top of the base. This is to create the hanger.

What's in it for the children?

Children can explore their own creativity, whilst also practising following simple instructions.

Taking it forward

- Make other types of windchimes with shells, sticks, old cutlery and compare their tunes.

Observation questions

- Does the child select tools and techniques needed to shape, assemble and join materials they are using?

- Does the child make their own choices?

Splash art

Expressive arts and design

What you need:

- Aprons and newspaper
- Large canvas
- Mud
- Paint
- Plastic cups
- Paintbrushes
- Masking tape
- **Large pieces of card** (reuse cards that were used as display board background)

What to do:

1. Find a work space, ideally outside as splattering can get messy.

2. Set up the canvas, preferably lay it on a table, on the floor or mount the canvas to a wall.

3. Protect the surroundings of the work space with newspaper and provide aprons to cover the children's clothes.

4. Set up the mud paints by mixing mud/soil/soft clay with water. Thicker paints work best for splattering paint.

5. Limit the area of the splatter. If splatters need to only be on a certain portion of the canvas, use masking tape to surround that section, and cover up the remaining canvas.

6. Dip a brush in the mud paint.

7. Help the children to position themselves. Stand back from the canvas. Once children get started, let them experiment with how far they stand away from the canvas.

8. Splatter mud onto the canvas. With a quick whipping motion, bring the arm down towards the canvas, and flick the wrist.

What's in it for the children?

Children will be able to develop their gross motor skills while engaging in creative play. The wrist movement involved in flicking the brush is excellent preparation for developing writing skills.

Taking it forward

- Scooping: scoop up a small amount of mud paint with a plastic spoon, hold the handle of the spoon with one hand, and pull back the top of the spoon with the other hand. Then let go of the top of the spoon to sling shot mud onto the canvas.

- Straw blowing: dip one end of a straw into the mud paint. Bring the straw over to the canvas, and place mouth on the other (clean) side of the straw. Hover the straw about an inch above the canvas, and forcefully blow through the straw to transfer the mud from the straw onto the canvas.

Observation questions

- Does the child show enjoyment when engaging in artistic activities?

- Does the child use different senses when exploring materials?

50 fantastic things to do with mud and clay

Creepy crawlies

Understanding the world

What you need:

- Pictures of snakes, worms and other creatures
- Pieces of clay
- Water

What to do:

1. Look together at the pictures and talk about the shapes of the various creatures.

2. Explain that the children are each going to make one of the creatures. Cut or rip a chunk of clay off for each child, basing the size of clay on the size of creation the children will make.

3. Show them how to roll the clay out into a long snake.

4. Making a coil (or snake shape) is easiest when started in the middle and worked out to the ends.

5. The diameter of the coil is up to the children. Thicker coils won't break as easily, but longer coils are more fun to work with.

6. Once the coil is formed, begin making the worms and snails.

What's in it for the children?

Children will be able to gain information about their own environment, the world around them and other living beings.

Taking it forward

- Find out about other animals, insects and birds and make clay shapes to represent them.

- Try working with other natural materials to create nature pictures.

Observation questions

- Does the child talk about some of the things they have observed such as plants, animals, natural and found objects?

- Does the child talk about why things happen and how things work?

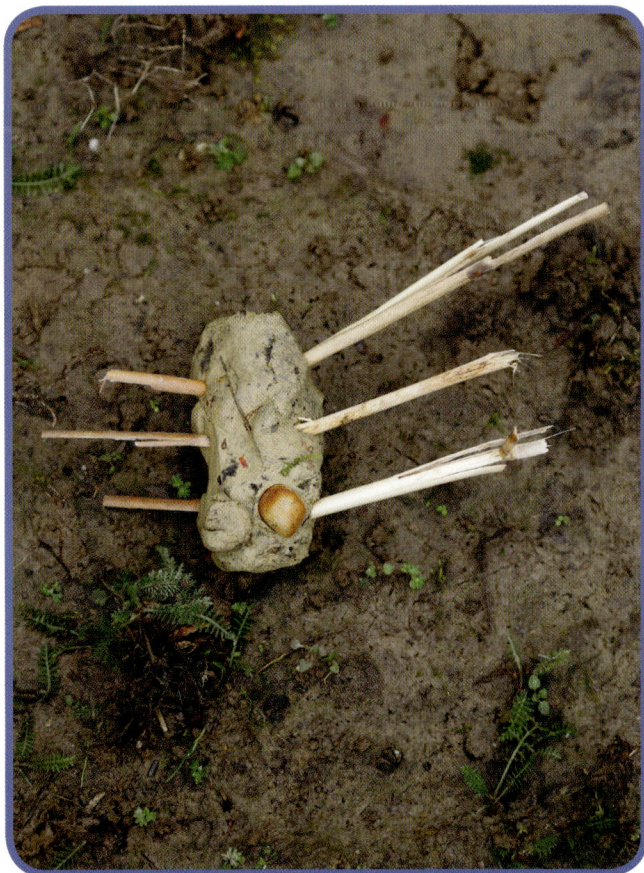

Minibeast chases

Understanding the world

What you need:

- An outdoor area with a variety of surfaces
- Some plastic pots, such as yoghurt pots, to put minibeasts in
- A paintbrush
- A magnifying glass

Log rolling

What to do:

1. Find a suitable outdoor area and make a clear map for the children to follow when they are on a walk.
2. Discuss the walk and what they might experience.
3. Carefully roll a log away to look underneath and see what's hidden – it's a good idea to do this with a friend so one can roll the log while the other is ready to catch any creatures.
4. It's not just minibeasts who like living under logs, so look for frogs and toads or newts, millipedes etc.
5. Use a paintbrush to gently coax the minibeasts into a pot – the paintbrush is far more delicate than trying to pick the creatures up with fingers!
6. Inspect your minibeasts with a magnifying glass, then release them back where you found them.
7. Discuss what type of soil the creatures live in.

What you need:

- A plastic funnel
- A jam jar or similar pot
- A desk lamp
- A magnifying glass
- Handful of leaves
- Soil

Mud litter creatures

What to do:

1. Place the funnel in the jam jar.
2. Put a few handfuls of leaves and some outdoor soil/mud litter from under some trees or bushes into the funnel.
3. Now position the lamp close to the leaf litter – but not too close (to avoid setting fire to the leaves).
4. A few hours later children should find a collection of tiny creatures in the bottom of your jam jar as they have tried to move away from the heat and the light of the lamp to find somewhere cold and damp.
5. . Look closely with the magnifying glass and children may find all sorts of tiny creatures.
6. Make sure you release the minibeasts safely back into the undergrowth.

50 fantastic things to do with mud and clay

What you need:

- Lots of collection pots, such as yoghurt pots, to put minibeasts in – a clear, plastic bug pot with a magnifying lid will help to get a close up of any creatures found

- A white sheet such as an old bed sheet or pillow case

- A stick

- A tree or bush

- Paintbrushes

- Magnifying glass

Bush-bashing

What to do:

1. Find an outdoor area with trees and bushes.

2. Spread out the sheet on the ground under the tree or bush.

3. Give a branch a firm shake or a hard hit with the stick – taking care and watching out for others around!

4. Use the paintbrush to gently put the creatures that fall out of the tree or bush into the collection pots to have a closer look with the magnifying glass.

5. Release the creatures back onto or at the base of the tree or bush.

What's in it for the children?

Children will learn about other creatures whilst also learning about their own limitations, and they will understand how their own decisions might affect the life of other beings.

Taking it forward

- Make a minibeast mud-hotel.

- Make a photographic minibeast guide.

Observation questions

- Does the child show interest in their environment?

- Does the child compare different places in their life (home-nursery-nanny's house for example).

- Can the child operate simple equipment?

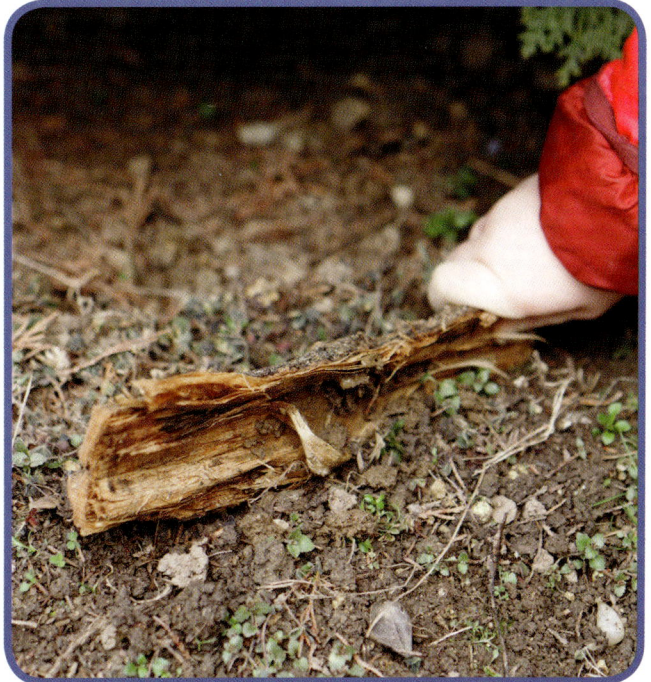

Tree spirits

Understanding the world

What you need:

- Pieces of clay
- Leaves, sticks
- Natural embellishments

What to do:

1. Cut or rip a chunk of clay off for each child. The size of clay broken off will determine the size of tree spirit children will make.

2. Roll the clay into a ball and flatten slightly.

3. Pat the disc onto the tree trunk.

4. Create a face shape using the sticks and use natural additions such as leaves to complete the details of the face.

5. Ask each child to name their spirit.

What's in it for the children?

Children can learn about the world around them using their investigation and observation skills. Noting characteristics and small details such as the patterns on different tree barks, the shapes of different leaves and so on will help children in developing observation skills, memory and navigation.

Taking it forward

- Make other clay animals that might live in muddy areas, such as pigs in the farm mud, shells in the river mud.

- Explore where clay could be found in nature.

Observation questions

- Does the child talk about some of the things they have observed such as plants, animals, natural and found objects?

- Does the child talk about why things happen and how things work?

Soil collecting trip

Understanding the world

What you need:

- An outdoor area with exposed soil surfaces
- Buckets or other small containers
- Small spades
- Microscope

What to do:

1. Find a suitable outdoor area and make a clear map for the children to follow when on a walk.

2. Discuss the walk and what they might experience.

3. When on the walk ask children (who are old enough to tell) to describe their experiences.

4. Use the small spades to collect samples of the soil from various surfaces. Place them in the buckets or other containers and take them back to your base.

5. Observe the samples under a microscope, encouraging the children to describe the textures they can see.

What's in it for the children?

Children will have the opportunity to pay attention to less obvious details that will help the development of their observation skills, their ability to focus and prioritise.

Taking it forward

- Observe different types of 'indoor dirt' such as chocolate cake crumbs, sand, playdough, flour and so on under the microscope.

- Make a soil map of the local environment.

Observation questions

- Does the child talk about some events in their own lives?

- Is the child co-operating? Is the child ready to share information?

50 fantastic things to do with mud and clay

Clay nest making

Understanding the world

What you need:

- Pieces of clay
- Water
- Natural nest-building material such as sticks, leaves, feathers

What to do:

1. Observe images of nests with the children during circle time, and discuss the ways in which animals might prepare their nests.
2. Cut or rip a chunk of clay off. The size of materials used will determine the size of the creation children will make.
3. Roll the clay out into long snake, then curve it into a coil.
4. Once the coil is made, begin making nests by curling the coil into a semi sphere.
5. Add additional materials such as sticks, feathers and leaves to the clay base, just as birds would in the wild.

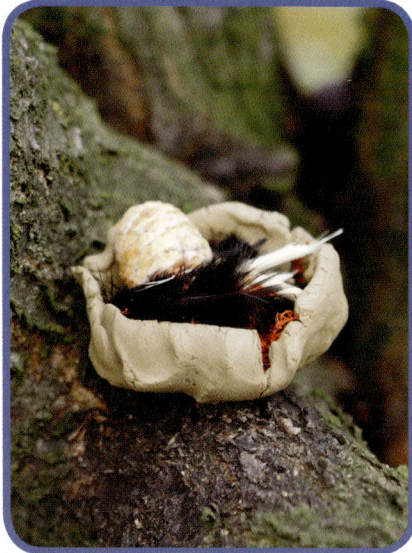

What's in it for the children?

Children will understand that we share the planet with other living beings.

Taking it forward

- Make clay animals to populate the nests.
- Organise a nest-spotting trip.

Observation questions

- Is the child talking about things they have seen or experienced?
- Can the child talk about things in the environment of their home?
- Does the child make comments?
- Does the child ask questions?

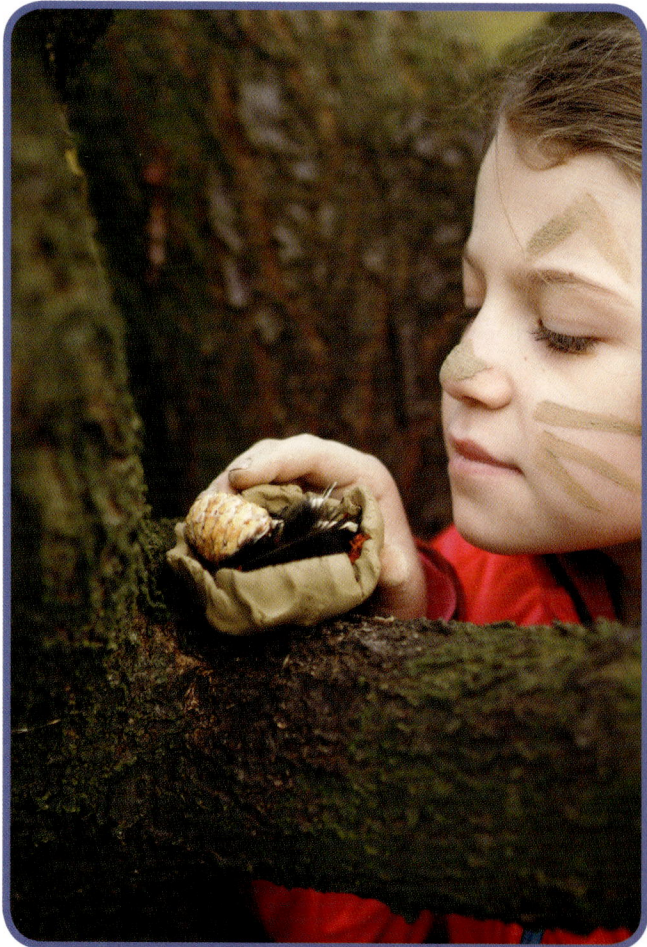

50 fantastic things to do with mud and clay

Sensory mudbath

What you need:

- A large paddling pool
- Water source
- Swimsuits for the children
- Glitter
- Flower petals
- Organic oil for smell/bath salt (optional)
- **Mud as desired** (moor mud is a good choice)

What to do:

1. Fill the pool with warm water.
2. If desired, add several drops of organic essential oils or bath salts to the water for fragrance.
3. When the tub is filled with water, add your mud of choice, ensuring it is clean and ideally free of chemicals. If you are prepared to purchase your mud, 'moor mud' is a good option.
4. Break the mud clumps up with your hands and swish them around.
5. Ask children to slowly get into the pool and immerse their whole body, except for their head, in the muddy water.
6. Allow them to soak and play for no more than 20 minutes, and then drain the pool.
7. Rinse the children off with warm water and hand out towels for drying off.

What's in it for the children?

Children will learn how they connect to nature and why is it good for them.

Taking it forward

- Organise a flower-foraging trip for samples to use in the bath.
- Build a beauty or spa salon scene for imaginative play.

Observation questions

- Does the child show interest in their own body, their physical being within the natural world?

Health & Safety

The children will need to wear swimsuits to participate in this activity so talk to parents first to make sure this is acceptable and practical. Check for any skin allergies or sensitivities before trying this activity.

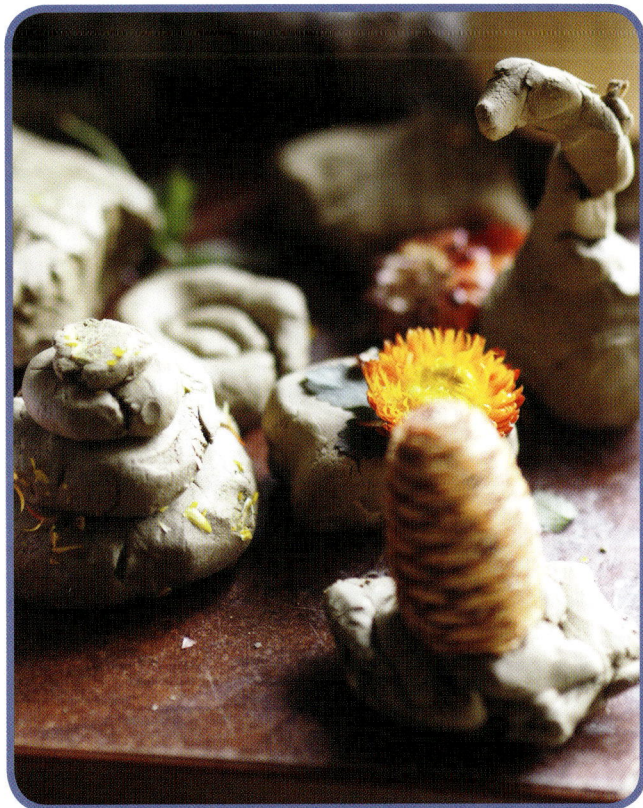

Soil treasure hunt

Understanding the world

What you need:

- An outdoor area with exposed soil surfaces
- A collection of different small rocks, pebbles, leaves and twigs
- Buckets or other small containers
- Small spades
- Magnifying glasses
- Microscope
- **Camera** (optional)

What to do:

1. Find a suitable outdoor area and make a clear map for the children to follow when on a walk.

2. Discuss the walk and what they might experience. Use the children's existing knowledge about their local environment.

3. Show the children a collection of rocks, pebbles, leaves and sticks.

4. When on the walk ask children to collect similar items themselves.

5. Encourage them to pick up whatever they find to be a treasure in the mud or soil. Remind them to make sure not to affect the environment negatively e.g. only collecting fallen leaves rather than pulling them off the trees.

6. Ask the children to lay out the collection during circle time. Study and compare the samples and try to group the rocks, pebbles and additional items based on characteristics such as colour, size, texture and so on.

7. Observe under a microscope and with magnifying glasses.

8. Alternatively, create a specialist local geology map, by placing photos of the samples on the prepared map, referring to the spots where they were found.

50 fantastic things to do with mud and clay

What's in it for the children?

Children will understand that things in the world represent different values to different people, so they will develop an ability to respect the opinions and belongings of other people.

Taking it forward

- Organise a treasure exhibition where the children can present their collected items.

- Make a themed collecting day featuring pirates.

Observation questions

- Is the child excited about the findings of others?

- Does the child seek to acquire basic skills in technology (to turn on or off the equipment)? Is the child keen to use technology?

Mud-history

Understanding the world

What you need:

- Paddling pools or large containers
- Dirt (sand, soil, mud)
- Water
- Buckets
- Pictures or paintings of old mud roads
- Toy cars
- Welly boots

What's in it for the children?

Children will be able to use their skills to work in groups, negotiate, and express their thoughts. They will be able to practise taking on a variety of roles such as leader, builder, baker and so on.

Taking it forward

- Visit a museum to view artefacts from the past.
- Make a mud oven or mud fire pit.

Observation questions

- Can the children work as a part of a group and show understanding and co-operation?
- Can the children follow instructions?
- Do the children display verbal negotiating skills?

✚ Health & Safety

Ask children to wear old clothes or cover up their own and to wear welly boots.

What to do:

1. Discuss how people have used mud throughout history and how they have benefitted from its properties.

2. Talk about the lifestyle in olden times and look at pictures or paintings of old roads, buildings and even cooking facilities where mud was used.

3. Divide the children into small groups and help them plan how to make a useful object from mud.

4. Make a historical village plan and act out the life of a villager.

5. Find large containers or use paddling pools to create giant mud pits.

6. Let the children add dirt/soil and water until they are happy with the consistency of the mud.

7. Set up the container in a fairly open space. This is important so that stray mud doesn't find its way onto things it shouldn't be on.

8. Encourage the children to try to run toy cars in it to experience how it might have been driving on an old unsurfaced road.

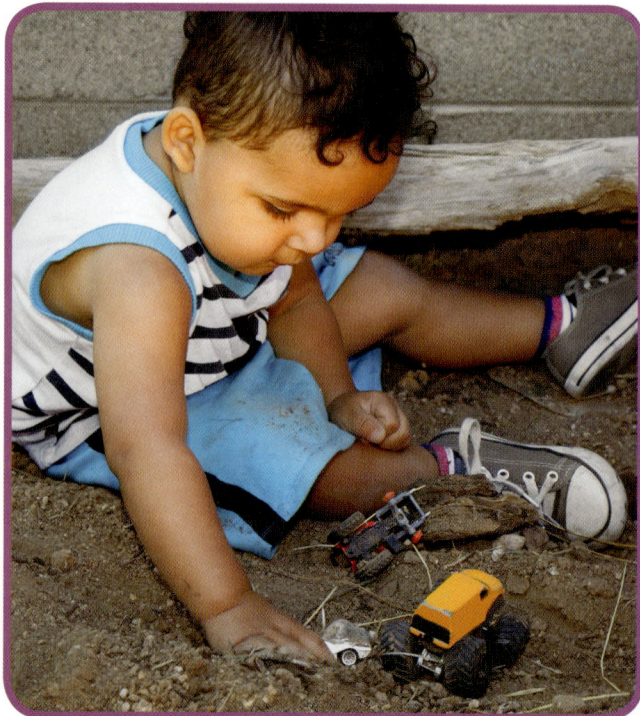